Asia

By Allan Fowler

Consultant
Nanci R. Vargus, Ed.D.
Primary Multiage Teacher
Decatur Township Schools, Indianapolis, Indiana

Children's Press®
A Division of Scholastic Inc.
New York   Toronto   London   Auckland   Sydney
Mexico City   New Delhi   Hong Kong
Danbury, Connecticut

Designer: Herman Adler Design
Photo Researcher: Caroline Anderson
The photo on the cover shows the Himalaya Mountains.

Library of Congress Cataloging-in-Publication Data

Fowler, Allan.
   Asia / by Allan Fowler.
     p. cm. — (Rookie read-about geography)
   Includes index.
   Summary: A simple introduction to the continent of Asia, including
its geographical features.
   ISBN 0-516-22234-1 (lib. bdg.)   0-516-25980-6 (pbk.)
   1. Asia—Juvenile literature. 2. Asia—Geography—Juvenile literature.
[1. Asia.] I. Title. II. Series.
DS5 .F69   2001
950—dc21
                                    00-057037

The biggest pieces of
land on Earth are called
continents.

There are seven continents.

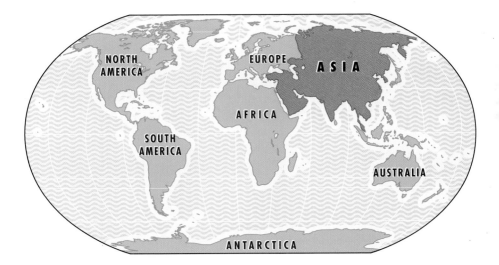

Asia (AY-shuh) is the biggest continent in the world. It has the most land and the most people.

More people live in Asia than in all the other continents put together.

You can find Asia on a globe. Asia is far across the Pacific (puh-SIF-ik) Ocean from North America.

On a map, Asia and Europe (YOOR-up) look like one continent. But Asia is a separate continent.

NORTH AMERICA

North Pole
+
ARCTIC OCEAN

EUROPE

Black Sea

Caspian Sea

Dead Sea

Tundra

A S I A

Yellow River

Yangtze River

Himalayas

Ganges River

AFRICA

PACIFIC OCEAN

Equator

INDIAN OCEAN

North

West ✦ East

South

AUSTRALIA

9

Asia has many different kinds of land.

Tundra (TUN-druh) covers most of the top, or north, of the continent. Tundra is frozen ground.

Some animals, such as reindeer, can only live on the tundra in the summer.

13

Evergreen forests
grow below, or south
of, the tundra.

Wide grasslands are
also found there.

Some parts of Asia are
very dry, such as this
sandy desert.

Other parts of the
continent are covered
by tropical rain forests.

Big rivers flow through Asia.
The Yellow River is in China.

Many people live near India's
Ganges (GAN-jeez) River.

Many kinds of animals are
found in Asia. Apes make
their home in the rain forest.

Pandas live in the Himalaya
(him-uh-LAY-uh) Mountains.

The Himalaya Mountains
are called "the roof of the
world" because they are
so high.

The highest and lowest places on Earth are found in Asia.

Mount Everest (EV–uhr–ist), in the Himalayas, is the highest.

The lowest is the Dead Sea. This saltwater lake is saltier than the ocean.

The salt makes it very
easy to float!

There are many different places in Asia. But in one way they are all the same. They are part of the biggest continent on Earth.

Great Wall of China

Words You Know

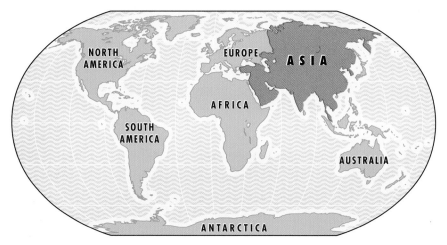

continents

ape

Dead Sea

desert

globe

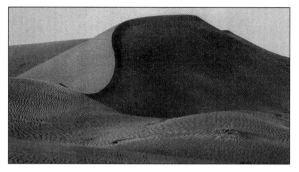

Himalaya Mountains

panda

rain forest

tundra

Index

About the Author

Allan Fowler is a freelance writer with a background in advertising.
Born in New York, he now lives in Chicago and enjoys traveling.

Photo Credits

Photographs ©: China Stock/Liu Liqun: 15; Corbis-Bettmann: 16, 31 top left
(Arthur Thévenart), 18 (Julia Waterlow/Eye Ubiquitous), 13 (Staffan Widstrand);
International Stock Photo/Orion: 29; Nance S. Trueworthy: 6, 31 top right;
Network Aspen: 5 (Jeffrey Aaronson), 24 (Rebecca Green); Stone: 21, 31 center
right (Tim Davis), 19 (Michael Harris), 10, 31 bottom right (Pal Hermansen),
20, 30 bottom left (Renee Lynn), 17, 31 bottom left (James Martin), 27 (Hugh
Sitton); The Image Works/Jon Burbank: 14, 23, 31 center left; Viesti Collection,
Inc.: cover (Andy Selters), 26, 30 bottom right (Duby Tal/Albatross).

Map (p. 3, 30) by Bob Italiano.
Map (p. 9) by Joe Le Monnier.